YOU'RE LOVED, DAD

A FEW REASONS WHY

Hallmark
GIFT BOOKS

Copyright © 2011 Hallmark Licensing, Inc.

Published by Hallmark Gift Books,
a division of Hallmark Cards, Inc.,
Kansas City, MO 64141
Visit us on the Web at www.Hallmark.com.

All rights reserved. No part of this
publication may be reproduced,
transmitted, or stored in any form or
by any means without the prior written
permission of the publisher.

Writer: Laura VanZee Taylor
Editor: Chelsea Fogleman
Art Director: Kevin Swanson
Designer: Scott Swanson
Production Designer: Bryan Ring

ISBN: 978-1-59530-344-8
BOK3121

Printed and bound in China
FEB12

To My Father,

You know how much I love you, right? I hope so, and I hope you know how important you are in my life. But in case you need a little reminder, here's a book with a few reasons why I am so glad you are my dad.

Love

Lisa   Krissy   Steve

I love you, Dad:

- ☒ For the times you said, "Go for it."
- ☐ For the times you said, "No way."
- ☑ Because, duh, you're my dad . . .

    . . .(Visualize eye rolling here for old-times' sake.)

Thanks, Dad:

☒ **For the advice and all those little "life lessons" you gave.**
                (I was listening even if I didn't act like it.)

☐ **For the times you didn't say anything and let me learn for myself.**

☒ **For just being there.**

Dads are something kids never outgrow.

I want you to know, I'll never stop being your kid, even when I'm:

having my own kids, 100 years old, independently wealthy

I love you, Dad, for all that you have done for me. I could never thank you for it all.

One thing that I want to thank you for is:

Never adding on to my disappointment when I've made mistakes

Coming to all of my softball + volleyball games ☺

Being the perfect example of what a father should be.

Dad, I love you for the things you've said a billion times (like "it's different" "anyone want to go do something"), for your stories, and, yes, even for (or in spite of) your jokes.

One of my favorite Dad-jokes or stories is:

When you skipped around Kansas in an applehat with us

At Gustavus, when you were talking about how great your "rubbers" were and I turned around and saw you on the ground.

When you stepped on poop in TJ Maxx.

If you were a TV dad, you'd be most like:

- G ~~☒~~ Charles Ingalls from "Little House on the Prairie"—full of strength and spirit.
- L D ~~☒~~ Eric Taylor from "Friday Night Lights"—inspiring the family team.
- S ~~☒~~ Cliff Huxtable from "The Cosby Show"—making everyone laugh.
- ☐ Red Forman from "That '70s Show"—you call it like you see it.
- K ~~☒~~ Cameron Tucker from "Modern Family"—nurturing and devoted.
- ☐ Tim Taylor from "Home Improvement"—if it's broke, you can fix it.
- ☐ Homer Simpson from "The Simpsons"—D'Oh!

Dad, I'm proud of all the things you do well.

I'm grateful you taught me how to:

drive a car (instead of mom :))

put-up Christmas lights 🎄

Be a good listener to my children

We've had some good times together, haven't we, Dad?
Remember when

used to go to Hardees before school and eat

raison buscuits with extra frosting

- We watched 7th Heaven every Monday Night
- I'd make you rub my head

we went to just about every pro sports championship ever!

Super Bowl, World Series x 2, and Stanley Cup Finals complete with tour of the Met Center basement!

One of my favorite traditions with you is...

~~I'm grateful you taught me how to:~~

christmas eve breakfast / watching old home movies

Christmas eve breakfast

Listening to you read "Twas the Night Before Christmas" to my boys on Christmas Eve.

As my father, you've been my:

- ☒ Landlord
- ☒ Fund Manager
- ☒ Taskmaster
- ☒ Coach
- ☒ Role Model
- ☒ Teacher
- ☒ #1 Fan
- ☒ Friend
- ☒ and my *tour guide*

As your kid, I've been your:

- ☒ Adorable joy
- ☒ Pain-in-the-neck (sorry about those teen years)
- ☒ Student
- ☒ Financial burden (thanks again!)
- ☒ Sidekick
- ☒ Personal laugh-bringer
- ☒ #1 Fan
- ☒ and your _#1 teaser (we tease the ones we love)_

I love you for the times you've helped me. Whether it was with my home-work, a problem, or with learning something new.

Thanks for helping me:

get out of trouble when I've been overwhelmed.

Helping me "perfect" school projects with late-night trips to Kinkos. I especially remember you making transparencies for my Cold War project b/c it wouldn't all fit on my floppy disk.

Through many challenges, most meaningfully, through some of the mental crisis I've faced.

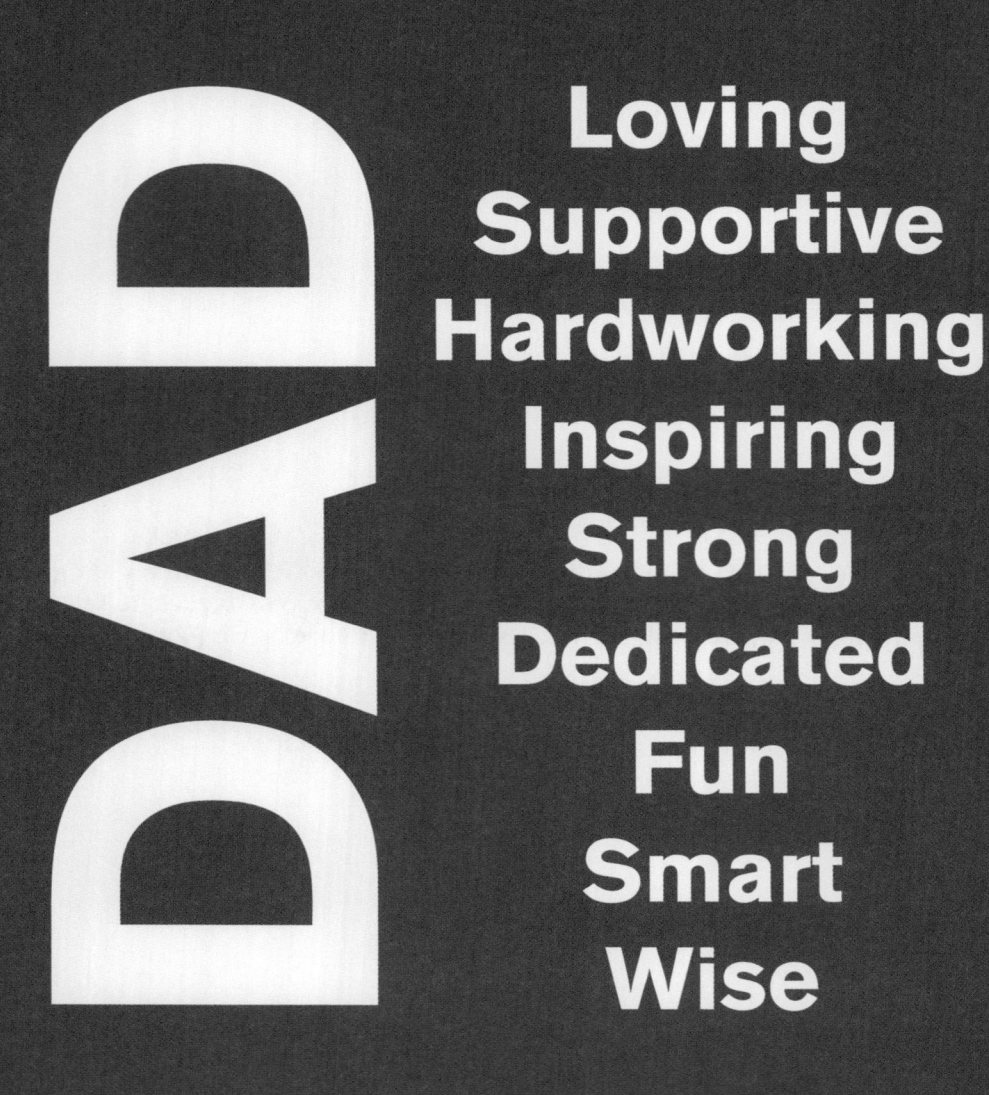

DAD

Loving
Supportive
Hardworking
Inspiring
Strong
Dedicated
Fun
Smart
Wise

If I had to describe you in three words, they'd be:

Caring   Honest   Energetic

Generous   Honest   Dorky

Devoted   Selfless   Compassionate

I love you for what you taught me about life—the wisdom you passed on to me from your experience.

One trait I am so grateful I got from you is...

~~Thanks for helping me:~~

Your compassion for others

Your dorkiness (and honesty)

Concern for others' feelings

Thanks, Dad, for always reminding me to:

- ☒ Be myself
- ☒ Think before I speak
- ☒ Work hard
- ☒ Have fun
- ☒ Take risks
- ☒ Aim high
- ☒ Walk, not run
- ☒ ~~~~ check Costco first

You Can Do It!

Practice Makes Perfect!

Try, Try, Try Again...

Sometimes I needed a little push, and you were there.

I remember when you encouraged me to:

go back to school + try jobs until I figure out what I want

upgrade to a large popcorn because its only 50¢ more

by your example, you have encouraged me to give humbly and anonymously.

Sometimes a hero is a regular guy who works hard to make life good for his family.

**For everything, Dad,
I love you.**

If I could wish anything for you, I would wish:

For you to be stress free and to enjoy each day

For you to be happy, healthy, + stress free... and to have a mattipoo farm.

For you to have some sense as to how much I love you for being the dad that you are -- just for all the wonderful character traits you have that make you such an unbelievable father.

If you have enjoyed this book
or it has touched your life in some way,
we would love to hear from you.

Please send your comments to:

Hallmark Book Feedback
P.O. Box 419034
Mail Drop 215
Kansas City, MO 64141

Or e-mail us at:
booknotes@hallmark.com